HOW
TO
SUrvive
JUNiOr
HiGH

HOW TO SURVIVE JUNIOR HIGH

Ann Hodgman
and
Patty Marx

Illustrated by
Mena Dolobowsky

Rainbow Bridge®
Troll Associates

Library of Congress Cataloging-in-Publication Data

Hodgman, Ann.
How to survive junior high / by Ann Hodgman and Patty Marx;
illustrated by Mena Dolobowsky.
p.   cm.
ISBN 0-8167-3033-4
1. Junior high schools—Juvenile humor. [1. Schools—Wit and
humor.] I. Marx, Patty. II. Dolobowky, Mena, ill. III. Title.
PN6231.S3H63   1994   818'.5402—dc20   93-40968

Published by Troll Associates, Inc. Rainbow Bridge is a trademark
of Troll Associates.

Printed in the United States of America.

10 9 8 7 6 5 4 3 2

INTRODUCTION

Everyone knows that junior high is the most wonderful time in a person's life. If *you're* in junior high, congratulations! You'll never be happier than you are at this exact moment. Right now you've got the most friends you'll ever have . . . you're the best-looking you're ever going to be . . . you've got the highest grades you'll ever get . . . and you love your family more than you ever will again.

What? What do you mean, "That's not true?" It's true for everyone *else* in junior high. What's the matter with you?

Oh, wait a minute. We started out with the wrong introduction. That paragraph was supposed to be in our *other* book about junior high, the one called *How to Hypnotize Yourself into Having a Good Time Wherever You Go.* The way we really meant to start out was like this:

Going to junior high school isn't easy. In fact, it can be tough. That's why you need our help.

Who are "we"? We're just regular people. But we *have* done a lot of research for this book.

There's a junior high school right in our town. Sometimes we walk past it and peek in the windows. Plus we flip through old teen magazines whenever we're in the library, and once Patty sat next to a seventh grader on the bus for almost half an hour.

Most important, we both went to junior high ourselves, and we're both still alive, or at least we think we are. So we must have done something right.

And whatever that something was, we're going to pass it along to you.

1

I DON'T THINK WE'RE IN ELEMENTARY SCHOOL ANYMORE!

HOW CAN YOU TELL JUNIOR HIGH FROM ELEMENTARY SCHOOL?

Remember that building you went to last year, with all those tiny desks and a crossing guard to hold your hand? Well, that was called your "elementary school." That's why it had all those pictures of squirrels and snowflakes in the windows. The school you're going to *this* year is junior high. That's why the cafeteria is such a mess.

Sometimes, new junior high students have trouble remembering where they are. Are you one of them? (Hint: Look around. Do you recognize the room you're sitting in?) Here are the best ways to tell the difference between elementary school and junior high.

1. Last year, the kids you shoved ahead of in line at the drinking fountain were very, very small. This year, the kids shoving ahead of you in line at the drinking fountain are very, very large.

And speaking of lines, in elementary school you *always* had to line up. In junior high, you *only* line up to get a drink of water. The rest of the time, everybody just mills around in the halls.

2. In elementary school, the teachers call kids "kids." In junior high, they call kids "people." But they still *think* of them as kids.

3. Last year, your homework was drawing oranges on a map of Florida or counting the number of pillows in your house. No wonder elementary-school kids like homework!

In junior high, you do not get to use crayons or markers when doing your homework, and the kind of counting you do can't possibly be done on your fingers. That's another difference. In elementary school, you could do the math. In junior high, you can't.

4. In elementary school, your parents help you with your homework. In junior high, they just yell at you because they don't understand it either.

5. In elementary school, you take sort-of-fun field trips to watch cows being milked. In junior high, the only trips you get to take are to places like the Town Hall so you can learn how local government works. Thrilling!

6. In elementary school, the school plays are called "Mr. Bigg's Garden" or "Benjamin Franklin's Wonderful Discovery," and everyone gets a part, even if it's only a tree or a dancing potato. In junior high plays, the only person who gets a part is Sandy Beckwith, who always gets *all* the parts.

7. Last year, your teacher said, "You won't be able to do that in junior high." This year, your teachers say, "This may be good enough for junior high, but it will *never* be good enough for college."

8. In elementary school, 5 percent of the girls are on a diet. In junior high, 5 percent of the girls aren't.

9. In elementary school, the boys have Band-Aids on their faces because they fell down on the blacktop during recess. In junior high, the boys have Band-Aids on their faces because they were secretly testing their dads' razors.

10. Last year, everyone was proud to say the Pledge of Allegiance. This year, everyone's embarrassed, especially the girls, who don't know where to put their hands anymore.

11. Last year, at the end of the day, the teacher would say, "I like the way Lia has her hands folded. Lia may get her coat and be first in line." In junior high, everyone just runs out the door when

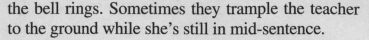

the bell rings. Sometimes they trample the teacher to the ground while she's still in mid-sentence.

12. In elementary school, you get to take turns washing the chalkboard, as though it's some kind of incredible privilege. ("Tommy, you've been so helpful today that you get to dip a mildewed sponge into cold, chalky water!") Who washes the boards in junior high? It's a mystery to us. Must be the blackboard elves up to their old tricks again.

Of course, some things about school never change, no matter how old you are. No matter what grade you're in, you have to study the New World Explorers every year. You're not allowed to chew gum in school. And if you bring your lunch from home, you never eat the fruit your mother puts in your lunch bag.

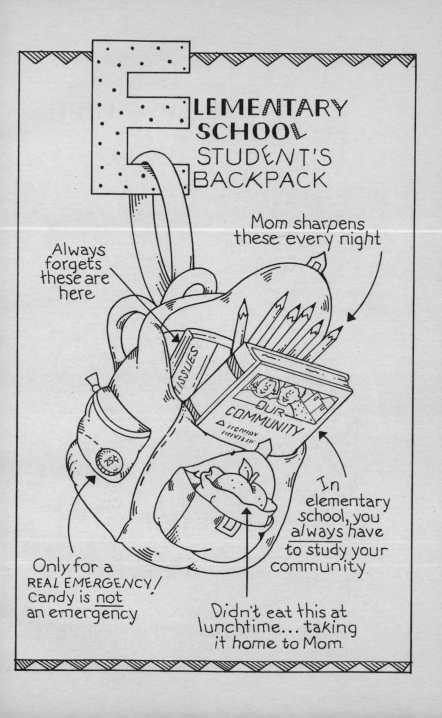

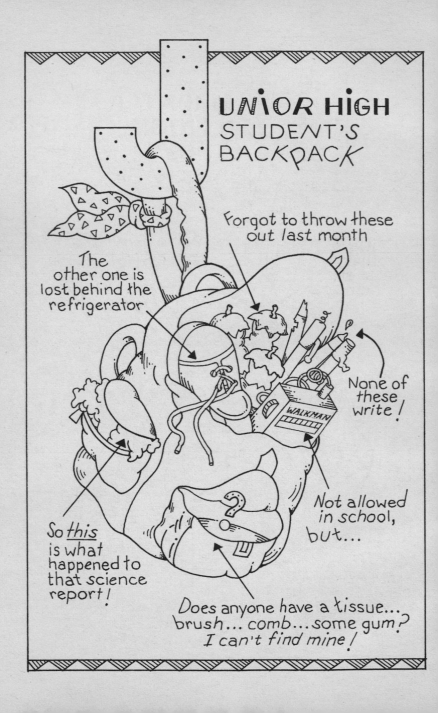

2

GETTING THERE: THE IMPOSSIBLE NIGHTMARE

A MINUTE-BY-MINUTE MORNING SCHEDULE

Most junior high experts agree that the worst thing about junior high school is having to go to it. Second-worst is waking up every weekday morning and knowing what's ahead of you. For lots of kids, hearing that alarm clock ringing in the morning is so depressing that they can't seem to get going even if their parents lie and say there are pancakes for breakfast. Lots of other kids don't even *hear* the alarm clock and have to come to school still wrapped in their blankets with their hair all funny.

What's the solution to this problem? A schedule! Following a morning schedule can help you find plenty of time to dress, eat breakfast, read the back of the cereal box, and fight with your sister. You'll feel a lot more in control. You'll get to school on time. Mornings will actually be fun again.

7:00 Alarm goes off. Keeping head under pillow, hit clock with blanketed hand. Clock will fall to floor, still ringing.

7:05 Your mother pokes her head into your bedroom and says, "Honey! Your alarm clock's ringing!" Mumble *"Ummmmmmmmm,"* keeping head under pillow and drooling slightly.

7:07 Fall out of bed onto alarm clock. This will stop the ringing and break the clock.

7:08 "Make" your bed by throwing a wadded-up ball of sheets and blankets onto the mattress, then hiding it all with the bedspread.

7:09 Open your eyes and look around a little bit.

7:10 Lie back down on your bed just for a *little, tiny second.*

7:20 Your little brother comes racing in and jumps on you. "Mom said to wake you up," he shouts, while pounding you very hard on the back.

7:22 Look in your closet. Find nothing to wear.

7:23 Stick your head out of your bedroom and yell, "Where is/are my blue sweater/jeans/socks?" "Look in the laundry," your dad will call back. Shout, "You mean it's/they're not even *washed* yet?" "Hey! You're old enough to do your own laundry!" your dad will call back.

7:25 Find some second-choice clothes. Struggle into them while lying on your bed with your eyes closed to catch a few more Z's. Actually fall back asleep. Catch way more Z's than you meant to.

7:36 Your little brother comes in and starts pounding you again.

7:40 Go into the bathroom to wash off the bloody nose your little brother accidentally gave you. At least it gets you out of your room. Once you've washed your face, you have no choice but to go have some breakfast.

7:45 Go into the kitchen and gloomily announce that once again, your little brother has totally *ruined* your day. No one in your family will look up from the newspaper/back of the cereal box/last-minute homework they're frantically trying to get done before the bus comes.

7:46 See nothing you want to eat. Gloomily announce that, too.

7:47 Your mother asks, "Why don't you have some cereal?" "Not this one," says your sister. "I'm reading it."

7:48 Find the only box of cereal on the table that someone is not reading. Pour a few pieces into your bowl. Realize that those few pieces were the only cereal left in the box.

7:49 "No fair!" your little brother howls. "Why should she/he get to finish all the cereal?"

7:52 Drink some juice. Eat the three or four pieces of cereal in your bowl with your hands. You don't need to use a spoon since your family finished all the milk before you got downstairs.

7:54 Suddenly realize how late it is. Accidentally swear because you're surprised. Get in trouble.

7:56 Race to the downstairs bathroom to brush your teeth. Shout "Hey, get out!" at your little brother. He will reply, "No! I have to *go!*"

7:57 Run to the upstairs bathroom to brush your teeth. Use your parents' horrible-tasting sensitive-teeth toothpaste, since yours is all gone.

7:58 Frantically try to rinse out the taste of that toothpaste.

8:00 Go downstairs and try to find your backpack.

8:06 Finally find it under the kitchen table, covered with G.I. Joes. Your little brother was using it.

8:07 Run out the door just as the bus pulls away.

8:08 Slowly go back inside to tell your parents you're going to need a ride.

See how much better a schedule makes everything work?

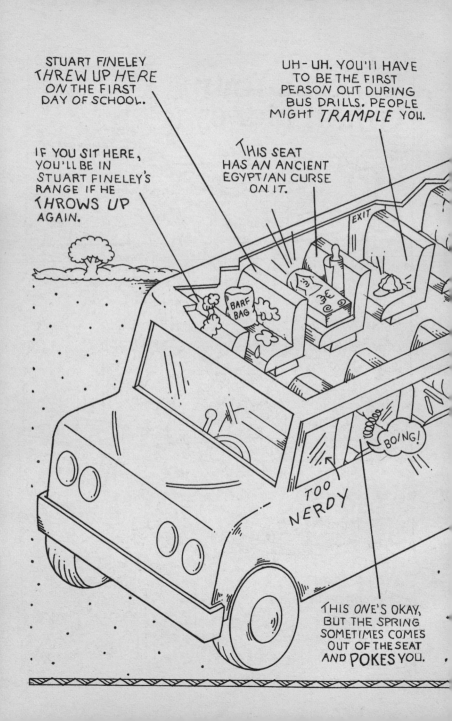

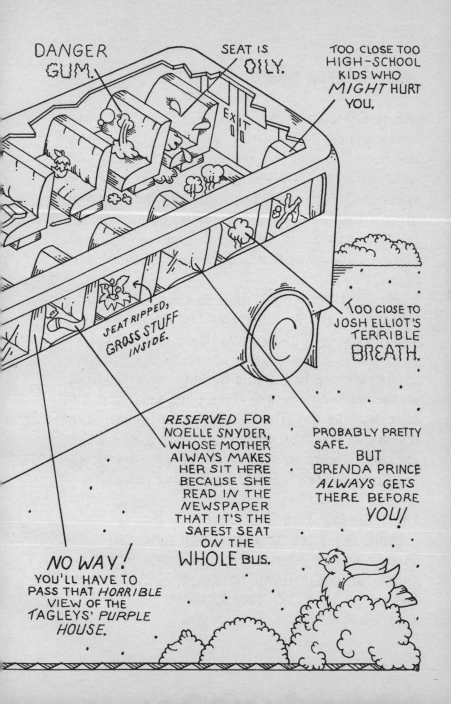

WHERE TO SIT ON THE BUS

Where *not* to sit on the bus is more like it. Almost every seat on a school bus has some kind of "bus cooties." The seat behind the driver? Makes you look like a goody-goody, plus it's a great target for spitballs. The seat way at the back of the bus? Not great if the bus stops suddenly and you happen to fall through the emergency door out onto the road and get run over by hundreds of cars. Wouldn't you agree?

We've given you a map to help you decide where to sit. But we think you'd be safer if you had your dad drive you — or just stayed at home.

Not everyone has trouble figuring out where to sit on the bus. Some people occupy the same seat day after day after day. The bus driver, for instance. But just in case you think the bus driver has it easy, we're enclosing a letter we came across (okay, we stole it), written by Sibley's School Bus Supply Company.

Dear School Bus Driver:
Well, it's that time of year again. Summertime is over, and bummertime is here. School's about to start, and you'd better be READY. The kids you drive

have had a full two months to dream up new ways of torturing you. This school year promises to be tougher on bus drivers than ever!

Luckily, we at Sibley's School Bus Supply Company are always ready to assist you with your driving needs. From reinforcing the seats in your vehicle (so they'll withstand hundreds of kids jumping up and down on them) to providing secret trap doors (so you can eject that weasely little Ross boy onto the road). . . to fitting your ears with special plugs (designed to filter out 90 percent of the screaming voices you hear every day). . . it's all here at Sibley's.

Come pay us a visit soon. We think you'll be surprised at our variety. Here are just a few of the new items in stock this fall:

• Sterile canister of pre-spat spit. Now you can wing spitballs right back at 'em!
• Bus-shaker. Easily installed on your dashboard. Kids too noisy? Shake 'em around a little — that will calm 'em down right away!

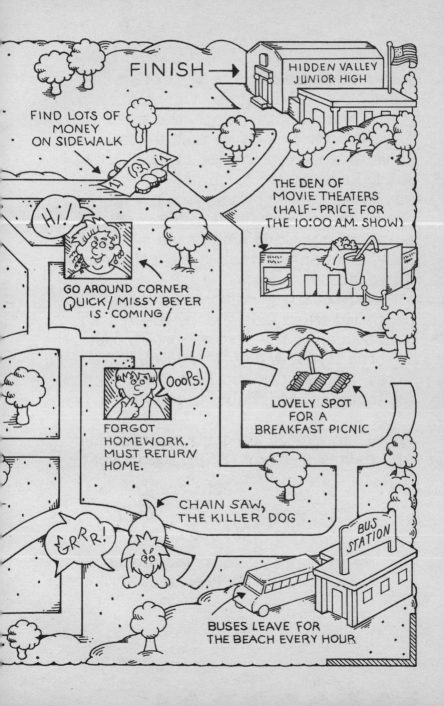

- Pair of glasses for the back of your head. Your "passengers" will think you're watching them ALL the time.
- NASA's invisible force field to circle the driver's seat. You can get in, but THEY can't. Protects you from paper airplanes, rubber bands, and flying straw-wrappers. Plus, it temporarily paralyzes any kids who brush against it, providing you with added pleasantness on your ride.
- Posters of scary bus accidents that happened when kids got too rowdy and didn't listen to the driver. Posters come in three styles: Mildly Frightening, Very Gross, and Get Out the Barf Bags (suitable for high-school use only).

There's lots more. So come on in! Enjoy! And have a pleasant, SAFE school year.

Sincerely,

Buster Sibley

Buster Sibley
President

3 THE WHY OF JUNIOR HIGH: YOU ARE PART OF A PROUD TRADITION

WHAT THEIR TEACHERS SAID ABOUT THEM

At this point, you may be starting to wonder something. It's probably along the lines of, "But you still haven't told me why I have to go to junior high! Why *do* I?"

Good question! The reason you have to go to junior high . . . uh, the reason you have to go to junior high . . . uh . . . oh, yes. The reason you have to go to junior high is that it is *traditional* to go to junior high. And you're a proud part of that tradition!

Throughout history, kids just like you have gone to junior high. Well, not all of them were just like you. Some of them were famous; some of them were infamous; some of them were totally ignored by history. But they all had one thing in common: teachers. That's not *one* thing, exactly, but you know what we mean.

And all of their teachers had comments about them, just the way your teacher has comments about *you*. For example:

George Washington

"George is an honest boy and a natural leader. He was elected class president this year. He is also the head of the Agriculture Club—but oddly, he cannot seem to stop himself from chopping down all the trees the other members of the club have planted."

Louisa May Alcott

"She would do a lot better in school if she didn't make up stories all the time. Also, her insistence on calling seventh-grade girls 'women' is very irritating."

Peter Pan

"Peter has a vivid sense of imagination and fun. He loves to wear tights so he volunteers for all the plays. Though he is quite bright, I am afraid that *once again* his immaturity will not allow me to promote him to the eighth grade."

Mona Lisa

"Very patient and has a lovely smile. But sometimes I get the feeling that Mona is in a world of her own."

Marie Antoinette

"Marie has nice manners, but she finds it hard to sympathize with others. She is reluctant to share things—especially her desserts—and spends more time planning her wedding to the future King of France than studying. Let's hope she can keep her head through all the festivities."

Zeus

"Zeus will make an excellent leader of the gods if he can only learn to be more *patient*. He has already thrown lightning bolts at seven students, vaporizing six of them. Also, his constant pranks—turning himself into a bull, for instance—are getting tiresome."

Michael Jackson

"Which one is Michael, again? I can't seem to remember what he looks like from one day to the next."

AMAZINGLY TRUE JUNIOR HIGH SCHOOL FACTS FROM HISTORY!

1. The words *junior high* come from the ancient Greek *torja haburi*—which means "place of torture"!

2. Before backpacks were invented, junior high students had to carry their books in their cheek pouches!

3. There was once an assembly at a junior high in Concord, Massachusetts, that was so boring a student fell asleep and couldn't be awakened for four months!

4. Before the nineteenth century, you did not need a signed parent's permission slip to go on a field trip!

5. The same fluorescent lights at Camden Junior High in Maine have been on continuously since 1914, which is why the Camden Junior High football team is known as the Washed-Out Wizards!

6. If all the sticks of chewing gum ever chewed in all the junior highs were laid end to end—before they were chewed—they would circle the earth ten times!

7. So many nurses enlisted in World War II that Wisconsin's Baraboo Junior High was forced to hire an orangutan as a school nurse!

8. In 1961, a seventh grader named Maria Alpert used a *ballpoint* pen on a standardized test instead of a Number 2 pencil!

9. At Brighton Junior High in Rochester, New York, Mr. Sherbinkski's sixth-grade English class read *Where the Red Fern Grows*—and not one student cried!

10. *Every single kid* at Nonnewaug Junior High School is popular!

THE JUNIOR HIGH SCHOOL TIMELINE

The next time you're having trouble in junior high, just take a deep breath and think about all the many, many junior high school students who came before you. Some of them had trouble, too. But you don't hear them complaining about it, do you? Come on, get with the program!

1,000,000 B.C. A school of fish tries to form a junior high, but they are swallowed up by a giant sea serpent.

45,000 B.C. A Neanderthal woman tries to set up a one-cave junior high, but it is too dark. All the students leave before Miss Ug finishes carving her name on the wall of the cave.

3813 B.C. The first homework assignment is given in Mesopotamia: "Come up with three uses for the wheel."

3201 B.C. In Egypt, Cheops Tutkemon builds a pyramid in shop.

423 B.C. Greeks design the first gym outfit. They call it the toga. They celebrate by having gym and calling it the Olympics.

235 The first pop quiz is given in Rome. Everyone flunks because no one has learned Roman numerals yet.

750 The Dark Ages begin. Lots of kids play hookey, but it is so dark that their teachers don't notice.

1034 Lady Godiva rides on horseback to school without any clothes. She is the first student to be suspended for breaking the dress code.

1424 Romeo passes a note to Juliet during study hall, asking her to go steady.

1620 Native Americans and Pilgrims celebrate the first Thanksgiving. Kids celebrate the first Thanksgiving vacation.

1773 Colonists rebel against the English by staging the Boston Tea Party. Seventh graders in Boston rebel against the teachers by staging the Boston Food Fight.

1815 Elijah Rutherford is the first eighth grader to get detention for chewing gum in class.

1822 Principal Harrison of DooDad Junior High comes up with the idea for the first "up" staircase. The problem is that there is no "down" staircase, so everyone is stuck on the second floor.

1849 The California gold rush begins. Cathy Forman and Glen Simons, seventh graders at San Francisco Junior High, pan for gold in the water fountain.

April 12, 1861 The Civil War begins.

April 13, 1861 Mrs. McGrath is the first history teacher to ask on a test, "What were the eight causes of the Civil War?"

1871 The Great Chicago Fire. A record number of kids get yelled at for talking during a fire drill.

1877 Thomas Edison patents the record player. *Party!*

1879 Shelly Kelly is the first teenager to have her own telephone. However, she has no one to call.

1912 The student council of George Washington Carver Junior High is the first student organization to sell peanut brittle.

1924 Roger Toohey shoots the first straw onto the ceiling.

1928 Irving Roberts is the first junior high student to put chalk inside the chalk erasers.

1928 Irving Roberts is the first junior high student to dunk a girl's braids in ink.

1929 Irving Roberts is the first junior high student to blow up a science lab.

1930 Irving Roberts is the first junior high student to end up in jail.

1951 Millie Presburg and Todd White become the first junior high couple to get their braces stuck together while kissing.

1971 The first girl named Shawna appears.

4

YOUR LOCKER AND YOU: FINDING YOUR WAY AROUND SCHOOL

OUR GIFT TO YOU — A COMPLIMENTARY SCHOOL MAP!

So you've finally made it to junior high. Are you lost yet? In elementary school, no one gets lost. For one thing, you are hardly ever allowed to leave your classroom in elementary school. This is not so bad because there is nowhere exciting to go in elementary school, unless you call a long hallway exciting. And on the rare occasions that you are allowed to venture into the world outside your room, you have to hold the hand of your "buddy" and follow closely behind the other pairs of buddies.

Junior highs, on the other hand, are very complicated places where they let you navigate on your own. It is impossible not to get lost at first. But don't worry—97 percent of all students who get lost in junior high find their way . . . eventually. What becomes of the other three percent? We think they may be wandering around the incinerator room in the basement.

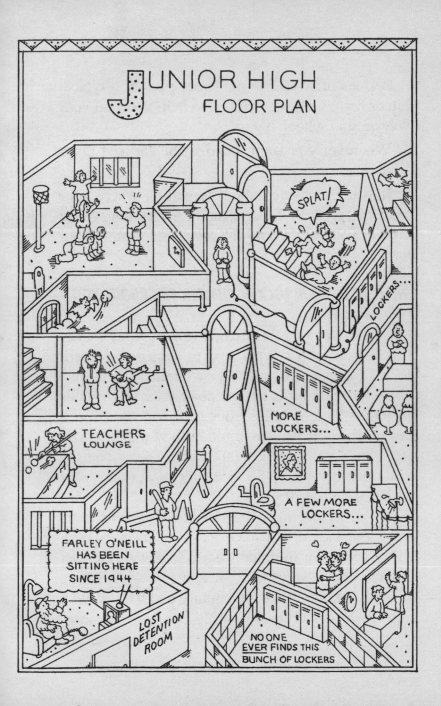

Besides offering this *free* floor plan of a typical junior high, we have two tips to help you find your way around school:

1. Wherever you want to go is the farthest point from where you are.

2. If you are worried about forgetting where your locker is, try this: Tie one end of a very long string around your locker and the other end around your wrist.

WHAT DOES YOUR LOCKER NUMBER SAY ABOUT YOU?

Chances are, you don't think about your locker much. You wish it were next to someone *decent's* locker for a change, and that's about it.

But your locker is really one of your best friends in junior high. It holds your stuff for you, it gets really smelly if you leave rotten food inside it, and its sharp door-corners scrape against your shins if you open it too fast. So next time, don't take your locker for granted!

In the olden days, before stealing had been invented, kids didn't have locks on their lockers. (That's why, in the olden days, lockers were just called "ers.") Nowadays, of course—when crime stomps through every community and it's not even safe to blink anymore—kids can lock up their mildewed gym clothes and chewed pens and know that they'll be completely safe.

Your locker combination is an even better friend than your locker, because it reveals things about your life that you never knew or even wanted to know. For example:

Odd number: Tomorrow you will miss the school bus.

Even number: Don't wash your hair tonight.

Number is divisible by three: Wear an extra pair of socks tomorrow.

Number contains one zero: Beware of friends named Zed.

Number contains more than one zero: You are *such* a loser!

Repeating digits: You will do everything twice today.

Digits add up to a number greater than six: You like to have fun.

Digits add up to a number less than six: The answer to the sixth question on the music test is "C."

Digits add up to six: Your best friend is a spy from Outer Mongolia.

Number starts with one: You will grow up to be President of the United States.

Number is the same backward as forward: You will go far in life.

Combination contains a letter of the alphabet: Someday you will read a book with that letter in it.

Number is negative: Forget it!

MAKE YOUR LOCKER SAY "[YOUR NAME HERE]"!

Lots of kids in junior high think lockers have to be drab, gray rectangles that all look the same, except for a dent or two where somebody kicked them. That's not true anymore, thanks to Locker Logos— a company that designs artwork, gadgets, paraphernalia, and other junk especially for lockers.

Just to show you some of the many possibilities for custom-designing your locker, we are reprinting a page from the Locker Logos catalog. To order, write to Locker Logos yourself. Unfortunately, we don't know their address.

1. You may not be Scarlett O'Hara, but that doesn't mean your locker can't look like Tara. Two columns and a porch are all it takes to turn your locker into a Southern classic.

2. Worried about theft? Well, you don't have to worry anymore with Loud Locker, the world's first security system for—yes—lockers. The instant anyone besides you touches your locker, a loud voice that sounds like the principal's booms, "Hey, you! That's two days detention!"

3. Hot enough for you? No sweat. Your locker can be as cool as an ocean breeze when you install air-conditioning. This summer, everyone will want to hang out by your locker! Comes with kerosene-powered generator.

4. Safety first! Avoid locker injuries. Get an airbag for your locker! Approved by the AAA.

5. Brrrrrrr! That's what people will say when they see your "igloo" locker. Simply stick on the ice-block decals. Also available: hole for ice-fishing. Fish and Arctic foxes sold separately.

THINGS YOU CAN STORE IN YOUR LOCKER

Your entire wardrobe
Your CD collection
Video games

A small television
A mobile phone
Posters and artwork
Some throw pillows
A blow dryer and hair mousse
Ferns
Raisins
Freeze-dried snacks
School books (if you have room)

THINGS YOU SHOULD NOT STORE IN YOUR LOCKER

Popsicles (unless you live in Antarctica)
Birds (alive or dead)
Livestock (alive)
Freshly cut flowers
Camembert cheese
Rotten eggs
Plutonium
Priceless jewelry
Your locker combination (if you have not memorized it yet)

WHAT TO DO WHEN YOU FORGET YOUR LOCKER COMBINATION FOR THE FIFTIETH TIME, AND LAST TIME THE OFFICE TOLD YOU THAT WAS THE ABSOLUTE LAST TIME THEY WERE GOING TO GIVE YOU THE COMBINATION AGAIN

1. Move to another state.

2. Convince your parents to educate you at home.

3. Share Betsy Carter's locker for the rest of the year. Of course, you'll have to persuade her to leave her blue-cheese-smelling track shoes at home.

4. Figure out a way to come in through the back.

5. Get very skinny so you can go through the slits in the top.

6. Get Batman to take time off from making his next movie and help you out.

7. Try to convince the office for this *one absolute I-promise-it-will-really-be-the-last* time. Like this:

"But it's really not my fault this time, because I was just pulling the lock-thingy off and suddenly someone slapped me on the back and I mistakenly closed the lock up again while my head was hitting into the hard metal of the locker, and the impact must have made me forget the combination."

5

HOME, SWEET HOMEROOM—OR, WHERE HAVE ALL MY BEST FRIENDS GONE?

SAMPLE NOTES

Face it. You'll never get through junior high without passing notes. They're the only way to keep in touch with your friends now that you're all in different classes. They're the only way to look as if you're paying attention when you're really writing down all the reasons you think the kid sitting next to you is cute. And in boring classes, they're the only way to save your life. Without them, you might fall asleep and never wake up again.

Basically, there are three kinds of notes. On the following pages you will find some representative samples. If you don't have time to write a note today, you can use one of these. Trust us. No one will notice.

The I'm-So-Bored Note

Dear Nina,

Right now Mrs. Baranoff is telling us about how earthquakes form along fault lines. Like I really care! This class is sooooo boring. Here are some things I would rather do instead of listening to Mrs. Baranoff: listen to static, watch dust collect, fold laundry for the whole world, go out with Perry Skully, ETC! You get the point.

Mrs. Baranoff just sneezed. She even sneezes boringly. I AM SO BORED!

Speaking of Mrs. Baranoff... don't you think she's looking awfully DIFFERENT lately? I keep looking at her stomach to see if she looks you-know-what. Do you think she is? Do you think if they hire a substitute it will be someone not so boring. Probably not. Is this <u>boring</u> or what?!

Will period 6 ever end??? Do you think if I call 911 they will come and rescue me?

Boredly,
Lynne

P.S. George Hornig said "Hi" to me in the hall (2nd floor) after 3rd period!!!

The I'm-Mad-at-You Note

Dear Randi,

You <u>may</u> have been wondering why I've been avoiding you lately. Wherever you were looking for me, I wasn't there. Like yesterday when I wasn't at your locker to walk home like we usually do. Or if you called me (I don't know if you did because I haven't been bothering to answer the phone) you would have noticed that I wouldn't have wanted to talk to you. Well I have to tell you that I'm really mad at you Randi. I don't want to hurt your (supposed!) feelings but I am.

It is <u>so unfair</u> how you have been talking to Madeleine Haywood when you know we agreed not to be friends with anyone from the Snob Mob. They think they run the whole school !!!!!! Well they don't and I am really surprised that you would waste your time with someone like that. Because she is a phony Randi you know that we agreed that she is. She probably doesn't even like you anyway.

and it is very stupid of you to go home with her after school every day when we always used to walk home from school together and I have a new Fanci Flowers kit I wanted to do with you. But I bet Madeleine thinks Fanci Flowers kits are so babyish or something.

Anyway Randi so that's why I've been staying out of your way. If you come back to your senses, you know where to find me. Waiting by your locker, like always.

Your (mad) friend,
Julie

The Interrupted Note

Notewriting can be risky. There's always the chance that your note will be intercepted and fall into the wrong hands. So most people learn how to stop quickly, hide their notes, and start again when they get the chance. Of course, it's sometimes kind of hard to follow a note like that:

Dear ~

Sorry about that. Ms. Snair was
watching me just when I was starting
this. Oh, no, she's looking at

Sorry again. Ms. Snair picked that
<u>exact time</u> to start staring at me. Whoops,
class is starting! Gotta go.

(Later) Now I'm in math. Sorry about
this different pen - my other one got lost
when I was

Can't remember what I was about to say
'cause Mr. Dobin started giving me this really
weird look like he knew I was writing to
you. So anyway, what's new?

Now it's after lunch. I'm in study hall.
Sorry about the chocolate milk on this. That's
one good thing about this study hall, Mrs.
Franck never minds if you're writing notes
instead of doing

Note to readers: This letter was confiscated. It
never saw the light of day until we snuck it out of
Mrs. Franck's desk.

Special Bonus! We've Managed to Intercept a Teacher's Note!

To: Rita Underwood
Social Studies Department
Third Floor
Sheponawaug Junior High
Main Street
Norwell, CT
U.S.A.
Western Hemisphere
Earth
Solar System
Milky Way Galaxy
The Universe

Dear Rita,

It's kind of weird, if you think about it- I mean, what was there before the universe?

Anyway, SMP- 'Scuse My Philosophy! I'm sitting here in Current Events pretending to take notes on the students' real reports. And is it _boring_. Chris Denholm is telling the class all about what's going on with the Australian Parliament. Wow,

50

really fascinating! I'm so interested in what happens in a country that's like a bajillion miles away from here!

Do you think Chris Denholm is cute? Circle one: yes   no

Who is the cutest kid you teach?

I wish we had a different principal, don't you? I don't like Mrs. Steinhauser very much. She's kind of mean. Plus, I think <u>she</u> thinks I come to school too dressed up. I mean, excuse me! Like it's a big problem if I want to look nice? What does she want me to wear, <u>overalls</u>? I'm sure the kids would really do what I say if I were in <u>overalls</u>!

Speaking of kids, Chris Denholm is looking at me funny. Oops! Is my epidermis showing??????? Hee-hee! Oh, maybe I'm supposed to give him a grade now or something. Okay, Chris. Your grade is ... F! Hahahahaha!

Just kidding. Well, gotta go give a few more Fs! No, just kidding again. See you in the teachers' lounge - we can make a list of our favorite kids we teach, okay?

Miss ya !!!!!!!!!! Don't let social studies (Social STINKIES, I call it!) get ya down!

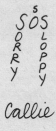

Callie

TIPS ON HOW TO WRITE AND SEND A NOTE

1. Never send a note along a route where it will pass by someone who is mentioned unfavorably in the note.
2. To prove that you have worked long and hard on a note, use at least three different pens. As you start to use a new pen, write "Sorry, my pen ran out of ink!"
3. Make lots of drawings in the margin so that if

you become a famous artist someday, your friends will be able to sell your notes for a lot of money.

4. Fold your note again and again until it is bite-sized. That way, if the teacher asks you if you are sending a note, you will be able to pop it into your mouth.

5. If you do get caught sending a note by your teacher and the note contains something mean about your teacher, prepare to flunk that course.

6. Never underestimate the stupidity of your reader. Therefore, as you write a note and come to the end of a page, write "over" in big letters. For added security, you should draw an arrow indicating that the reader must turn the page.

7. When your teacher is not paying attention, rig up a pulley system between each desk in your classroom. This will make it much easier to pass notes inconspicuously. If you drill two holes in the side of each desk (quietly—you don't want to get caught!), it will be a simple matter to attach a pulley. A pulley is a simple machine, like a ramp or a lever. You'll probably be studying them soon, and then you'll know how to make one. You have to do something with wire, we know, but we're not sure what exactly. Anyway, here's what your between-desk pulley system should look like:

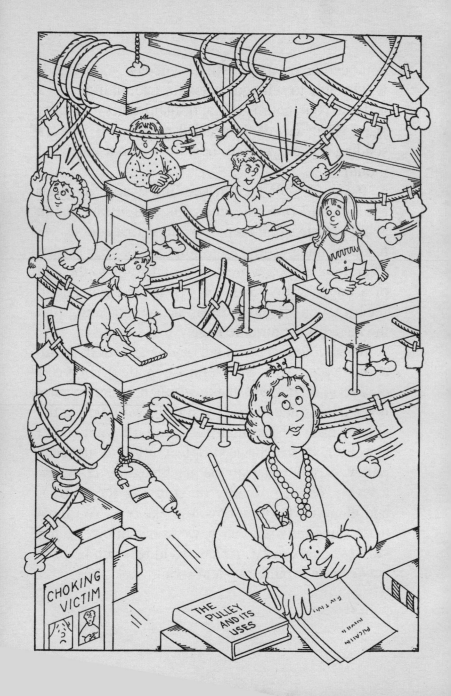

You are excused from this chapter. Your parents wrote a note. Please turn to the next chapter.

YOUR TELEPHONE AND YOU

For as long as there have been telephones (about five hundred years, maybe? We don't have time to look it up right now.), there have been parents complaining that their junior-high-age kids talked on the phone too much.

That just isn't true, as you know. The majority of kids in junior high don't talk on the phone nearly enough. Even so, the telephone is their most important appliance in the house. It's *way* more important than the stove, for example. In fact, most kids' problems would be solved if their parents would just take out the stove and have more phones put in the empty space.

"I can't live without my phone," confesses Emily Birnbaum. "It's connected to one of my major arteries." That's because Emily had a cordless phone surgically attached to her wrist in seventh grade. But even kids who aren't as lucky as Emily agree that if their phones were taken away, they would die.

Sometimes kids who are just starting junior high

aren't sure how to talk on the phone. Oh, they can make quick calls to have a thousand pizzas delivered to Mr. Fullbright's house—you know, easy stuff like that—but they still don't know how to answer the phone like a real junior-high-schooler.

So we've provided a handy sample call—between you and an imaginary friend—for you to practice with. Read it aloud a few times, and you'll get the hang of it. Only don't talk too loud, or your mother will get worried about you sitting alone in your room talking to yourself.

You'll have to pretend you're a girl (if you aren't one)—a girl named **A** with a best friend named **B**. Maybe those aren't the most interesting names in the world, but we don't have time to make up names right now either.

A: Hi, it's me. MOM, WILL YOU CUT IT OUT? I JUST GOT ON THE PHONE THIS EXACT SECOND! My mother is having a total cow already.

B: Yeah, mine too. She was actually talking about making me *set the table*. Can you believe it? So what are you doing right now?

A: Talking to you.

B: I know *that*, stupid. I mean, what're you doing *besides* that?

A: (sighs gustily): My stupid math. It's so hard.

B: Yeah, really. I thought it was, too.

A: (shrieking): You're DONE already? How did you get done so fast? I'm so stupid! I'm only on number 5!

B: Oh, I couldn't get that one at *all*. I mean, what do they think, we're in *college?* I asked my dad to help me, but he just, like, started yelling about what are they teaching us in school. Standard parent garbage.

A: Parents are so gross, and they don't even know it. MOM, STOP IT! I'VE ONLY BEEN TALKING FOR THREE SECONDS! Sorry. My mother claims she needs the phone, like I really believe that. I'll believe it's an emergency when she shows me the blood.

B: So do you like Jeff Dorsett, or do you *like* like him? Because I think he's really, really cute. But, I mean, if you *like* like him I'll stop thinking it.

A: I do *kind* of *like* like him, I guess. Like the other day, he looked at me in the media center.

B: (shrieks): AAAAAAAAAAAA! No way! That is so cool! Like, *how* did he look at you? In a *meaningful* way?

A: No. Not really. More like he thought I was a fat pig.

B: Oh, he did *not* think that. I'm the one who's fat, anyway.

A: Yeah, right. You're as skinny as—MOM! THIS IS MY PHONE TOO, YOU KNOW! NOT EVERYTHING IN THIS STUPID HOUSE BELONGS TO YOU! I prob'ly better go soon. My mother is *literally* making me *throw up.* So what are you going to wear tomorrow? OKAY, MOM! I'M HANGING UP *RIGHT NOW*, IN ACCORDANCE WITH YOUR STUPID WISHES! My mother says there was an earthquake and the front of the house caved in. Yeah, right! So what are you going to wear the day after tomorrow? . . .

(And so on, forever.)

We can't really give you a good sample boy's telephone call. That's because telephone conversations between junior high boys are impossible to understand unless you are a boy in junior high. They are not spoken in English, but rather in a language that consists entirely of mumble, garble, and slurred *ummm-huhs*. A phone conversation between junior high boys lasts forty-five seconds at the most. If it were translated into English, however, it would last much longer.

Here's a transcript of a telephone conversation between Sam Sweeney and Robert Johnson:

Sam: Huhhu. Sss.

Robert: Unhunnuyh, bruhluh jermah muh?

Sam: Nah. Mebtommah.

Robert: Meb.

Sam: Uh-huh.

Robert: Ehn.

Sam and Robert's conversation was too long and complicated to discuss fully here. Basically, though, they talked about a basketball game they had both watched, wondered what they would do that weekend, and pondered the meaning of life.

SUPPLYING YOURSELF WITH—UH— SCHOOL SUPPLIES

HOW TO WASTE TIME WITH YOUR SCHOOL SUPPLIES

Use your magnifying glass to magnify this sentence. (3 minutes)

Sharpen your pencils until they vanish into thin air. (15 minutes)

Scrape all the paint off your pencils and repaint them with whatever color you choose. (2 hours, 20 minutes)

See how many pencils you can balance on top of your head. (6 minutes)

Build a pencil log cabin. (18 minutes)

See how fast you can take the lid off a bottle of glue with your feet. (13 minutes)

Count the number of pages in a spiral notebook to make sure you weren't cheated. (6 minutes)

Try to draw the perfect circle without using a compass. (4 hours)

Erase everything in your brother's notebook. (12 hours)

Make a collage out of Post-its. (28 minutes)

Cut a piece of paper into slivers. (46 minutes)

See how high an index-card tower you can build. (21 minutes)

Decorate your sweater with gummed-paper reinforcements. (3 minutes)

Take the gummed-paper reinforcements off your sweater. (1 hour, 4 minutes)

Using a protractor, measure the angles of *everything* in your room. (8 hours, 42 minutes)

Take apart a pen to see how it works. (4 minutes)

Glue together everything in the wastebasket. (3 hours, 21 minutes)

Using dividers, create an easy-to-use telephone book. (1 hour, 29 minutes)

Draw on an eraser; then erase the drawing with another eraser. (6 hours, 41 minutes)

Make your own graph paper by tracing from a piece of real graph paper. (34 minutes)

Color every square of graph paper differently. (2 hours, 56 minutes)

Teach yourself to print beautifully with your other hand. (2 days, 6 hours, 11 minutes)

See how many book protectors you can put on a

single book. (17 minutes)

Build a fishing rod from a pen, a rubber band, and a paper clip. (49 minutes)

Fish for a soft eraser in the sink. (3 hours, 2 minutes)

Punch holes (with a hole puncher) in a piece of paper to spell your name. (4 minutes)

Cover both your hands with tape, using only your mouth. (2 hours)

Build a "Leaning Tower of Pencils" by sticking the point of one pencil into the eraser of another pencil. And the point of *that* pencil into the eraser of another pencil. And so forth. (19 minutes)

Design some paper-clip jewelry. (1 day, 1 hour)

Crochet a bookmark from rubber bands. (3 hours, 12 minutes)

Paint your toenails with rubber cement. (7 minutes)

Fill your pencil case with water, then clean up the mess. (16 minutes)

Perform a percussion solo with a few pens and a stapler; shake up a box of thumbtacks for an added tambourine effect! (14 minutes)

See how many pieces of cardboard you can staple together. (2 minutes)

Using a staple remover, try to take apart your desk. (3 days)

Separate your supplies into those that can be microwaved and those that cannot. (12 minutes)

Figure out which school supply you would eat first if you were starving to death on a desert island. (5 minutes)

Pretend your stapler is a puppet and put on a show. (38 minutes)

Pack a shoe box full of rubbings from an eraser. Eventually the rubbings will congeal and mold themselves into a giant eraser in the shape of a shoe box. (approximately 100 years)

THE LEGEND OF THE ANIMALS' SCHOOL SUPPLIES

You didn't know animals went to school, did you? Well, they don't (and don't ask us to make that fish-school joke again, because we're not going to). Strangely enough, though, animals do have school supplies.

One old Iroquois legend explains it this way:

Many, many moons ago—in other words, a long time ago—a bunch of animals happened to see some kids going off to school with their new school supplies. "Look at all that stuff they have!" said

Squirrel, who especially admired one girl's pencil case. "All I have are a couple of measly acorns!"

"All I have is a bread crumb," said Ant. "And it's heavy. I need a book bag."

Before long, all the animals in the forest were in a rage because they had no school supplies. And so they went to the lodge of the Great Spirit, who agreed to give them some school supplies of their own. However, he also gave them detention for bothering him.

First the Great Spirit gave a backpack to Kangaroo. The Great Spirit became slightly confused—it was his first time doing this, after all—and he put the backpack on Kangaroo's stomach instead of her back. But the Great Spirit did put some very pretty colored dividers in the pouch to make up for his mistake.

Next came Pelican. The Great Spirit gave the bird an Expando-beak to help him carry his stuff to school. However, he forgot to warn Pelican not to carry fish in there at the same time. Ever since, pelicans have had the stinkiest school supplies of any creature.

Hamster wanted an exercise wheel. The Great Spirit couldn't understand why a *wheel* counted as a school supply, but Hamster made such a fuss that the Great Spirit gave in at last.

To Owl, Great Spirit gave far more useful school supplies—sharp talons and eyes that could see through the darkest of nights. The talons were for catching mice for lunch. (Owls' schools are famous for their terrible lunches, so they have to catch mice to make up for it.) And the eyes? "You will be able to see the blackboard from two miles away," the Great Spirit explained. "But we don't *use* a blackboard," Owl whined. To this the Great Spirit replied, "Shut up and let the next animal in."

The next animal was Firefly, and you all know what the Great Spirit gave *her.* "Now you will be able to read under the covers and study very late at night," the Great Spirit told her. Firefly liked boys better than books, so nowadays she mostly uses her light to attract male fireflies. But the Great Spirit is sleeping then, so he never catches her.

To Octopus, the Great Spirit gave the ability to squirt great clouds of ink all over everything. "That's *kind* of like writing," the Great Spirit said helpfully. He could see that Octopus was a little disappointed, though, so he gave him eight arms to make up for it. "Oh, thank you!" Octopus exclaimed. "Now I can be on the gymnastics team!"

Saucy Woodpecker wanted to play tricks on his teacher. The Great Spirit gave him a sharp beak with which to make holes in the school walls. "Your teacher will think termites have been there. Perhaps she will even close school for a day," said the Great Spirit. "Ow! I didn't say you could peck *me!*"

Lowly Caterpillar was last in line. "I'm afraid you don't have anything left for me," she said mournfully. "I'm too ugly anyway."

"Yes, you *are* pretty ugly," the Great Spirit agreed. "But I have saved the best for last. Here is a cocoon. Hide in this if you have a test you don't want to take."

Caterpillar was delighted because the very next day she was having a grammar test on when to use "who" and when to use "whom," a subject she knew absolutely nothing about. When the teacher handed out the test, Caterpillar hid inside the cocoon. When she emerged, however, she not only had to take the make-up test, which was much harder than the first one, but she was also a butterfly and could not fit into her caterpillar clothes.

Moral: Even if you have good school supplies, life is not perfect.

HOW TO BLAME YOUR BAD GRADES ON YOUR SCHOOL SUPPLIES

School supplies can come in handy for lots of things besides . . . um . . . supplying your school. Here are a few examples:

You get 19 out of 20 multiple choice questions wrong on the history test. Well, it's not your fault. You put down some answers that you knew were wrong—as a sort of a joke. You were planning to correct your answers. But your eraser was so worn down that you had to leave the original answers.

You fail your geometry quiz. It's not your fault. Your compass is broken and your protractor is so old that it has obsolete angles and numbers.

Your English teacher claims you never even answered the last three essay questions on the test. It's not your fault—well, not exactly. You forgot and put invisible ink in your pen instead of blue ink.

Everyone has handed in a science project but you. It's not your fault. You built an excellent model of the entire universe—with a black hole and everything—but on the way to school it fell apart because your glue sticks were duds.

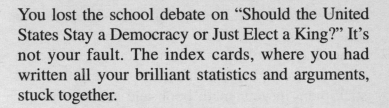

You lost the school debate on "Should the United States Stay a Democracy or Just Elect a King?" It's not your fault. The index cards, where you had written all your brilliant statistics and arguments, stuck together.

SCHOOL SUPPLIES OF THE FUTURE

A couple of centuries from now, junior high school students will have such great school supplies that you probably won't believe it. Isn't it horrible to think that you can't have them now? Maybe you can invent some way to freeze yourself and get thawed out in the future. It would make a great science project, too!

1. The Amazing Eyelid Adhesive—Painlessly keeps students' eyes open in even the most boring class. Comes in three sizes—Dull, Totally Boring, Might as Well Be Watching Grass Grow. Optional Neck Clamp keeps students sitting up nice and straight.

2. Flying Loose-leaf Binders—No longer will you have to drag home all those heavy books from school. Simply program your books and they will be home before you are.

3. Dividers That Really Divide—It's nice to organize your notebook, but wouldn't you really rather have book dividers that actually do some math for you? It is unclear how these work, but stick them in your math book and they'll do your homework!

4. Edible Erasers—Not only are these delicious, but once you've eaten them, you will never make a mistake again.

5. Rap Rulers—As they measure, they tell it like it is:

>"Inches are THREE!
>That's how it should BE!
>I'm a fine LINE!
>Hear me count to NINE!"

7
TERROR! TEACHERS! THE TERRIBLE TRUTH ABOUT YOUR TEACHER

Is your teacher an escaped convict? Probably. About 70 percent are. And that's not even counting the teachers who just spent a few hours at the station for a felony.

Often it is the nicest teacher, the one who looks the sweetest, who is the hardened criminal. Beware the teacher who smiles a lot: that teacher is simply happy to be out of jail. Look out for the teacher who says, "You kids are so great, there will be no homework." That teacher is probably on parole and knows that he or she will be back in jail too soon to worry about correcting homework.

Of course, teachers out on parole can also be the ones who give the most homework. They figure, "Those kids should suffer, too." Then again, a teacher out on parole might give an average amount of homework to fool you.

So how do you know for sure whether your teacher is an ex-con? Here are signs to look for:

Now, put this book down very slowly and casually. Tell the teacher you have to go to the bathroom. Then go ask the principal to call the police.

WHAT THEY TEACH TEACHERS

Of course teachers have to learn something before they can teach you, even if it doesn't seem that way sometimes. Most of them go to teachers' colleges, where they learn to read and write and do the other things they've forgotten over the years.

In addition to learning academic stuff, though, teachers also take classes in a few "extras." It may help you to know just what these extras are.

For one thing, all teachers learn to call students "people." No one knows why they do this. Some scientists speculate that the word "people" may once have meant, "Hey, listen up." Others point to an ancient superstition among teachers that saying "people" would make kids behave better.

When kids (*we* don't say "people," at least) act up in school, teachers learn *not* to jump up onto the desk and tear things apart. Instead, they're taught to cross their arms, eyeball the class in a mean way, and announce ominously, "I can wait." This is supposed to make the class calm down faster.

Actually, it helps to keep the *teacher* calm.

Teachers also learn secret skin exercises to help them detect the tiny breeze that a note makes when someone is passing it across the aisle. When your teacher is drawing a map of Italy on the blackboard, her skin is ever-alert for signs of note-passing danger.

Do you remember the day when you were playing with that poisonous snake in your desk and your teacher grabbed it and put it in *her* desk? During recess, you snuck into the classroom to try and retrieve Fang. To your surprise, you couldn't find him. Why? Because teachers learn how to build secret "confiscation drawers" into their desks that only they can find. A simple touch of the finger, and out slides the drawer—but only the teacher knows where to touch.

Teachers are also taught to talk about your "record" a lot. "That's going to go on your record," they like to threaten when you do something especially disruptive. Don't let this scare you! There *is* no such thing as your "record"—only a messy pile of papers stuffed into a grocery bag. The office will throw it all away when you get into high school.

Finally, at their graduation ceremonies, teachers have tiny computer chips embedded into their brains. These chips enable teachers to assign exactly the right amount of homework to prevent you from having time for fun at home. Right now we're working on a method for disabling these computer chips. As soon as we've perfected it, we'll let you know.

TEN SURE-FIRE WAYS TO DISTRACT YOUR TEACHER

1. Loudly whisper, "Did you bring the things for the surprise party?" just as class is starting.

2. Pretend that the floor is getting hot. Keep asking, "Mrs. Armstrong, doesn't the floor seem hot to you?" (If your teacher's name is not Mrs. Armstrong, substitute another name. If there is no floor in your classroom, substitute the ceiling.)

3. Have everyone in the class stare at the teacher's hemline so she will think her slip is showing. (If you have a male teacher, this may not work as well.)

4. Have everyone in the class suddenly burst into song.

5. *Earthquake!* Suddenly throw yourself onto the ground and begin writhing around.

6. Release a flock of turkeys or other large game birds in your classroom.

7. Ask the teacher distracting questions that will make him or her forget about teaching and just start talking about regular stuff. For example: *Who are you going to vote for? How long would it take to count to a million? How much did stuff cost when you were growing up? Is it true parents used to be stricter than they are now?* And our personal favorite, *If someone got sucked out of an airplane window, would they be dead before they hit the ground from all the air pressure and everything?*

8. Isn't it about time to have a florist deliver a great big bunch of roses for the teacher "from a secret admirer"?

9. Get your finger stuck in the class Venus's-flytrap.

10. Emit powerful eye-beams that will reach into your teacher's brain and scramble it like an egg.

A MEMO FROM THE SCHOOL NURSE

Why are we including a thing about nurses in the teacher chapter? Oh, come on, do you really expect us to write a whole chapter about *school nurses?* If that's the kind of mollycoddling you expect from us—well then, we're not even going to tell you our secret method for giving yourself a fever just by thinking about it. Besides, lots of kids in junior high spend more time in the nurse's office than they do in their own classrooms.

Date: September 5
To: All students of Shady Sky Junior High
From: Head Nurse Nife
Re: What You Should Know About the Nurse's Office

NURSE'S HOURS
The nurse does not work on Tuesdays from 11:00–2:00. If you expect to fall ill at that time, please wait or transfer to another junior high school.

HOW SICK DO YOU HAVE TO BE
TO BE SENT HOME?
Too sick to enjoy watching TV all day.

GYM EXCUSES
Any injury hidden by a bandage must be checked before a student will be excused from gym. If the injury has been drawn on the student's skin with Magic Marker, he or she will only be excused from

gym for the time it takes to wash off the ink with the nurse's special stinging soap.

FLU SEASON
This year, flu season is scheduled from December 15–February 21. Students who would like to participate must have at least three flu symptoms and a note from a parent. The nurse's office is proud to report that last year, our school won the Junior High Regional Flu Championship. Our average temperature was 102.3 (up 0.4 degrees from last year).

NURSE FANG
Do not be afraid if you are examined by Nurse Fang. She is an excellent nurse, no matter what she looks like.

FAINTING DURING CHOIR CONCERTS
The first three students who faint while singing in a choir concert will be treated nicely. After that, the nurse will suspect that you are faking it. The stage lights aren't *that* hot.

BROKEN FINGERNAILS
If a student's fingernail breaks and she was wearing nail polish, she will be allowed to remove the polish

and reapply a new coat in the nurse's office. If she was not wearing nail polish, she will just have to tape the nail together and hope for the best.

SPORTS AND CHEERLEADING INJURIES
Sports and cheerleading can cause injuries. Avoid becoming involved in these activities if you want the nurse to feel sorry for you when you get hurt.

CHICKEN POX
Junior high school students are expected to have had chicken pox already. Any students who catch chicken pox will receive a demerit for lateness.

WELL, YOU HAVE TO LEARN SOMETHING

THE MOST DISASTROUS SCIENCE FAIR PROJECT

Junior high students can learn a lot about science by participating in science fairs. For example, they can learn about the force of gravity when their booth at the fair accidentally falls down. They can learn about chemistry when they watch Merri Penfold's ray gun vaporize the judges. And they can learn about photosynthesis when the plant that was the main part of their experiment dies because it didn't get enough sunlight.

They can also learn about failure . . . and learning to start over again after you've failed . . . and then failing again. And that's a lesson you can't find in any science book, except maybe those science books that describe how alchemists in the Middle Ages tried to make gold.

Reed Nootley, Jr., gets the award for the most disastrous science fair project. The year before, Reed had received first prize at the science fair for

his discovery that tomato plants grow to an enormous size if they are fed lamb stew, baked potatoes, and chocolate-chip ice cream.

However, Reed's next project, "The Enormous Self-Peeling Banana," was less successful. Again, Reed fed his subjects a healthy diet. This time he gave them green beans, roast chicken, herbed rice, and stewed prunes with yogurt. Sure enough, Reed's bananas grew to an enormous size.

Then Reed put his enormous bananas under a sun lamp without first applying sunscreen. Reed's idea worked! Within a few minutes, the bananas peeled on their own.

Reed brought one of his Enormous Self-Peeling Bananas to the school science fair. Mr. Lipoff, the head of the science department, was about to award Reed first prize when a strange thing happened. The peel began to grow larger and larger. In a few minutes it covered the gym floor. Then it covered the entire school. Soon everyone in the school had slipped on the gigantic banana peel. No one could get up.

Eventually, the National Guard was called in to kill the banana peel and rescue everyone by helicopter. And Reed Nootley, Jr., gave up science.

A PAGE OUT OF HISTORY . . .

"Our Science Project,"
by Willy and Orvy Wright

For as long as junior high schools have been holding science fairs, the wrong kids have been winning first prize. Twenty years before they actually *built* the world's first airplane that worked, Wilbur and Orville Wright designed plans for a working "aeroplane" for the science fair at Dayton Junior High School, Ohio. Here are those plans, along with their teacher's comments.

This is a design for a piloted flying machine. We call it a "biplane." We think it will work, but we have not been able to test it because Papa would not give us money to buy the parts after we crashed our last model into the pigs' trough. The power for the aircraft is a 12 horsepower, four-cylinder engine fueled by gasoline. The aircraft is mounted on a small trolley fitted with two bicycle wheels on a wooden rail. This is how it will "take off."

[Teacher's handwritten comments:]
define!
Wrong term! A pilot is on a ship.
Should say "imaginary flying machine!"
↑ I don't blame him! What have horses to do with it?
arts & crafts?
define
???
— NO SLANG ALLOWED

There are three dials. One measures the ~~Engines do not revolt!~~
number of engine <u>revolutions</u>. One
shows the speed of the wind. The third
is a stopwatch so we can measure how
long the aircraft <u>stays aloft</u>. *arent you assuming a bit much?*
We think the aircraft will be able
to stay aloft for several seconds, *manifestly impossible*
perhaps as much as a <u>minute</u>. Of
course the speed of the wind will make
a difference. <u>Why</u>?

When we have finished paying
Papa to replace the pigs, we will
begin work on this model. It may
take us a long time, but we are
going to keep trying. ← *I wouldn't advise this.*

Boys,
   This is an exceptionally poor project.
Not only are your imaginations
<u>tremendous</u>ly out of line, but you offer
<u>no data</u> to back up your <u>exaggerated</u>
claims. If you are determined to tinker
with machines, why not stick to useful
machines, like mangles and apple peelers?

C-

P.S. You haven't even designed
    wings that <u>flap</u>!

HOW TO LEARN A FOREIGN LANGUAGE IN ONE MINUTE

As if English is not hard enough, many schools force you to learn another language. And they won't even count Pig Latin.

However, this isn't as bad as it may seem, especially if you have a language lab at your school. A language lab is a great place to listen to music tapes while pretending you're learning the story of how Pedro or Heinz or Pierre asks directions to the library or carries a suitcase or takes the bus. Listening to Pedro or Heinz or Pierre is supposed to help you perfect your accent. But here is an easier way:

1. Make the same funny face your language teacher makes.

2. Squinch up your eyes and talk through your nose.

One of the problems with language is tense. It's called that because that is how it makes you feel. In addition to the past, present, and future tenses, there are a lot of other tenses. Many of these have the word "perfect" in them, as in "the future perfect tense." We believe that if any of those tenses were *really* perfect, there would be no need for all the other tenses.

We also believe that it's silly to get too worried about using the correct tense. What is most important is communication. If you are in a foreign country, for example, you must be able to communicate what you want. If you use the wrong tense and have to wait a little longer to get what you asked for, just be patient. Remember—what separates the past from the present from the future is less than a second!

Now let's put some of these ideas into practice. We'll use the example of a junior high student named Tom Culligan, whose parents took him to Paris one summer. Tom really wanted to go to soccer camp, but his parents told him that he would never forget his summer in France. And they were right! Because here's what happened when Tom tried to use the French he had learned in junior high:

In a pastry shop

What Tom *thought* he was saying in French: "May I please have one of those lemon tarts over there in that tray?"

What Tom *actually* said in French: "Please, your eye will fell into my lemon. Very?"

On the bus

Where Tom *meant* to go: The Eiffel Tower.

Where Tom *actually* ended up: At a folk-dancing festival about twenty miles outside of Paris.

At a famous art museum

What the guard *really* said to Tom: "If you keep backing up like that, you'll knock over that priceless statue. Watch out!"

What Tom *thought* the guard was saying: "People from the United States are priceless. Welcome!"

How much it cost Tom's parents to replace the statue: More than it would have cost to send Tom to soccer camp.

When Tom returned to school in the fall

What he thought: That his French was much, much better.

What his classmates thought: That Tom was showing off.

HOW TO DO MATH

Why do you have to study math in junior high school?

"So you'll be able to keep up with the math in high school," teachers say.

"So you'll get into a good college," parents say.

"So all the math you'll ever need when you're a grown-up will be at your fingertips," liars say.

All *what* math you'll need when you're a grown-up? Grown-ups *don't* need math. They never use it. Grown-ups have calculators to do their addition and subtraction and accountants to do their taxes. Beyond that, they never think about numbers at all. And neither should you.

Luckily, there are only a few kinds of math problems. Solve them, and you can solve anything. Here's how:

Algebra Problems

"Jim is three times as old as Rachel. Next year, Jim will be four years younger than Rachel. If Jim's age = A and Rachel's age = B, how old are Jim's parents?"

How to solve it: First, break the problem down into its separate parts. The first part is *Jim is three times as old as Rachel.* So if Rachel were, say, four years old, then Jim would be—that's right, twelve years old! See, you're catching on already!

The second part of the problem is *Next year, Jim will be four years younger than Rachel.* Let's see— we already figured out that Rachel is four years old so that would make Jim *zero* years old next year, right? Which means he hasn't been born yet, so his parents are probably still pretty young. We'd guess that they're in their late twenties.

Geometry Problems

"Angle A = 60 degrees. Angle B = 60 degrees. Angle C = 60 degrees. What is the total number of degrees in this triangle?"

How to solve it: This is what they call a "trick" question. It's too easy—especially if you know that the angles in any triangle add up to 180 degrees. Obviously they want you to say 180. So you should fake them out and say *190*. That will show them that you're on your toes!

Problems with Pi

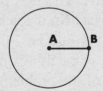

"AB is 4 inches long. What is the area of this circle?"

Okay. Another trick question. We're *supposed* to remember that the way to figure out a circle's area is to multiply pi times the radius squared. The thing is, though, that pi is a number that *goes on forever!*

So there's no way you can multiply *anything* by it. No one has a piece of paper that big. Whenever you see a problem with pi in it, you should just turn and walk off in the opposite direction, laughing sarcastically.

And here are three basic math facts you should keep in mind:

A small pizza has 6 slices. Mediums and larges have 8.

Trains are always late.

Three strikes, you're out.

THE ALL-PURPOSE BOOK REPORT

_____(name of book)
Webster's Dictionary defines (pick any word in title of book that is capitalized) as "_____" (definition). And that is truly what the theme of this book is about.

I really liked/hated the part when _____
_____(summary of second paragraph on page 67 of book). For me, this episode illustrated the theme, which is: good versus evil/learning to get along with your parents/how hard it is to find your way home if you are a cat.

The author cleverly uses language and theme, building to a moving conclusion. Characterization is used as well, delineating the different characters in the story.

In conclusion, this book, much like _____ _____(name of last book you read in English class), is for any boy or girl who likes adventure/a tale for all times/sitting in a chair for a long time. It can be located in the _____ (name of your school) media center.

To summarize, this book is certainly about _____(same definition as above). That is why I liked the book so much.

HOW TO DODGE THE BALL

For some junior high students, gym is the best part of the day. For others—like us—it's the absolute low point. When we were back in junior high, we hated gym so much that we still spend most of our time trying to get out of it.

If you actually like sports, you'll have to read about them in a different book. But if you're like us, you think that the worst thing about gym is having the ball come toward you and having to figure out what to do with it. This goes for *any* ball: volleyball, football, soccer ball, tennis ball. They're all your enemies.

So keep 'em away! Here's how:

Just as the ball reaches you, suddenly pretend you have to tie your shoe.

Ooops! A sneezing fit suddenly overcame you!

Try a little reverse psychology. Yell "*Here!* Send it *here!*" so loud that you scare your teammates away.

Just before gym, in the locker room, mention that your skunk perfume is activated whenever you touch a ball of any sort.

Politeness is always helpful. As the ball sails toward your hands, back away quickly. Smile and say, "Oh no, I've been hogging the ball all day. I'll let you have a chance!"

Let your teammates watch as you rub glue on your hands.

Persuade your gym teacher to allow you to take notes on the game so the school can have a record of this important gym class.

THE STUPIDEST SHOP PROJECTS IN HISTORY

Shop is a sort-of-good class because it's not really like a class. It's more like—well—*shop*. You get to make lots of fun presents for people, and you get to wear those nifty safety goggles.

Sometimes the projects get a little weird,

though. Here are the worst ever:

1. A wooden light bulb. Created by Andrea Reiffler. "I got tired of the way regular light bulbs burned out so fast. That'll never happen with this."

2. Digital dice. Created by Jason Walters. "Those 'dot' dice are so old-fashioned. I wanted something more in tune with today. The only problem is you can't throw these dice because you might break them. So you have to turn them over very carefully by hand. 'Course, that makes it easier to get the number you want!"

3. Full-size Dad-holder. Created by Scott Turnel. "When Dad gets tired, someone can just put him in here. It comes right up to his chin, so he can rest. But you have to be careful not to knock him down when he's in it."

4. Balsa-wood bookends. Created by Kevin Emmons. "Regular bookends are always so heavy. I wanted to give my mother something that would be a little easier to move around. Also, she can carry these in her purse if she wants to."

5. Nose rest. Created by Sheridan Fanu. "I noticed that my nose always gets tired before the rest of my face does. So now, when I'm doing my homework, I just pop my nose into this nose rest and I feel a hundred percent better!"

6. Metal Kleenexes. Created by Michael Woo. "These will save millions of trees. Millions!"

7. Door tote. Created by Deedee Pensley. "It's so hard carrying a door around! With this tote, it's a lot easier because there are handles so the door won't keep sliding out of your hands. I'm giving it to my grandmother for her birthday."

UH-OH! A POP QUIZ!

You didn't think we were mean enough to do this, did you? Well, we are. Don't worry, though—this test isn't a punishment. It's just a way of seeing how much you know. Yeah. Right. That's what teachers always say. But if they really want to know how much you know, why don't they just ask you?

Study the material in Chapter 8 carefully. Then, throw your book away so you will not cheat while taking this test.

The Test

1. A good title for Chapter 8 would be

    A. "Patty and Ann Write a Book"

    B. "Uh-oh! A Pop Quiz!"

    C. "Fun (Not Really) with Learning"

    D. "Why I Did Not Finish My Science Fair Project"

2. Match the historical figure with his or her accomplishment. Then draw a wiggly line connecting them.

A. Betsy Ross

a. First person to get yelled at for talking on the phone too long

B. Alexander Graham Bell

b. Sewed a flag to her skirt by mistake because she wasn't paying attention to what she was doing

C. Cotton Mather

c. Got grounded when she toilet-papered the principal's house during Halloween

D. Dawn Liddy

d. Didn't have anything to do with cotton

3. It's important to know a foreign language so that

A. You can read the menu in a foreign restaurant

B. You can show off to your parents in a foreign restaurant

C. You can order for your friends in a foreign restaurant

D. If you are ever in a foreign country, you can recognize the signs that say "Restaurant"

4. We wear safety goggles in shop class because
A. They look pretty
B. They protect our eyes from the sawdust that Phil Flanders is always spraying around
C. They make us realize what the world would look like if everything were orange
D. Our "compound eyes" see things the way insects do

5. The Wright brothers' teacher didn't understand their invention because
A. She was scared of heights
B. She was having a bad day
C. They were Wrong, not Wright
D. They wrote the description of the airplane in Cantonese, and she only spoke Mandarin

6. Even though cheerleaders' underpants sometimes show when their skirts fly up, it is all right because
A. They are athletes, and underpants are part of their uniform
B. No one is watching the cheerleaders anyway
C. It is all "good clean fun"
D. You should be ashamed even to think about a thing like that

7. Patty Marx and Ann Hodgman are
A. Talented authors
B. As glamorous as real models
C. The hosts of a popular talk show
D. Incredibly nice people

9 CLIP-AND-USE EXCUSES

HOW TO BREAK THE BAD NEWS ABOUT YOUR GRADES TO YOUR PARENTS

If you've been reading this book carefully, your grades are probably already 100 percent better. But let's say you're just standing in the bookstore flipping through the pages of this book, and let's say that in your backpack is a bad report card.

If your parents are like most, they will not be happy. In fact, they might even be so unhappy there will be some screaming, or grounding, or docking of your allowance. What are you to do?

First of all, stay calm. If you are nervous, you are likely to tell your parents the truth: that you deserved bad grades because you did not study and you never handed in your homework on time and your attitude toward schoolwork was not serious and you called your teacher a melon-head. But truth is not called for in this situation. We are not recommending lying (we would get in trouble with our editors for that), but there is such a thing as stretching the truth.

For instance, you could tell your parents that F stands for "Fine" and that D stands for "Darn Good." Or you could tell your parents that your teachers happened to be very strict this year and that everyone else got much lower grades than you. Make a graph showing that 25 percent of the class got G's in Social Studies and that Phil Muffler got a Z– in Spanish.

You might also try blaming your bad grades on your inadequate school supplies (see Chapter Six). Or you could pretend you were inexplicably blind all semester except when you were at home. If only you had been able to see the blackboard, you would have gotten all A's.

If excuses do not work, consider moving to another country. Peru has a lovely climate. Remember, your signed report card does not have to be returned to school for a week. That gives you plenty of time to pack. Of course, you may not want to move permanently to South America. Maybe you don't have enough luggage.

It's time to be brave—and lie. Just kidding. We really don't recommend lying. Someone would find out someday and then you could not run for Vice President. We think you should stand tall and present your parents with your bad report card. To make this easier, we have designed some clip-and-use consolation awards to give your parents along with your report card. Act as if these awards are a very big deal.

HOW TO WRITE YOUR OWN EXCUSES

Of course it's very wrong to write your own excuses instead of tricking your parents into doing it for you. Nevertheless, sometimes you *have* to come up with an excuse to get yourself out of school. Maybe it's such a beautiful day that you couldn't make yourself go indoors. Well, that's okay. We happen to think that you can learn just as much from nature as you can from Ms. Hardy's dumb old chemistry class. (Nature has chemistry *too*, Ms. Hardy!) All we want to do is help you get outside and learn it.

So here are some guidelines, plus a few ready-made excuses for when you're in a real hurry.

Guidelines
1. Do not sign the letter "Love, Mommy" or "See you soon, Daddy."

2. Do not use stationery that has drawings of animals on it.

3. Do not write in crayon.

4. Do not enclose money or gum.

5. Do not claim to have broken your leg unless you are prepared to wear a cast for three weeks or longer.

6. Diseases not to mention—bubonic plague (very rare in this century), hoof and mouth disease (only for cows), school-itis (does not exist).

7. It is inadvisable to write that your temperature rose above 105 degrees.

8. If you regularly use the "death in the family" excuse, keep a record. Remember—one person can have only one funeral.

9. The sickness of a pet is not recognized as a valid excuse for *your* missing school.

10. Avoid any mention of being kidnapped by alien beings.

11. When handing the excuse note to your teacher, do not say, "Please don't show this to my mom!"

Clip-and-Use Excuses

Dear _____ :

Please excuse _____ for missing school yesterday. He/She had a sore throat which the doctor said could be contagious. He/She feels okay today. However, if he/she feels contagious later on, I suggest you let him/her leave school early.

Yours,

_____

To whom it may concern:
I am sorry my son/daughter had to miss the math test yesterday, especially since he/she was really looking forward to the test. It seems that he/she was so excited about the test that he/she nearly had a heart attack. The doctor said it would be best not to give my son/daughter the math test **ever**. Actually, you should not give my son/daughter the history

quiz on Friday either.
Hope your heart is fine.

_____

Dear Mr./Ms. _____ :

I am sorry that _____
was not in school yesterday. A
burglar broke into our house the
night before and stole all our clothes.
All we had were the pajamas we were
sleeping in and _____ was too
embarrassed to wear pajamas to
school.
Truthfully,

_____

P.S. In case you're wondering, I
ordered the clothes _____ is
wearing today through a special
delivery catalog.

P.P.S. The burglar also stole _____'s
homework.

Hello there,

    I am sorry that _____ had to miss school all of last month. He/She had a dentist appointment.

    Really,

_____

Clip-and-Use Hall Passes

Name of student: _____
Date: _____
Time: _____
From: Homeroom
To: Roam the halls with no purpose in mind
Signed: _____

Name of student: _____
Date: _____
Time: _____
From: Latin
To: Spend the whole period pretending to be sick in the nurse's office
Signed: _____

Name of student: _____

Date: _____

Time: _____

From: Cafeteria

To: Hitchhike to the fast-food place, where only high-school kids are allowed to eat, and buy some lunch

Signed: _____

CAFETERIA ETIQUETTE

THE JUNK FOOD PYRAMID

Have you heard all that blab-blab-blab about the nutrition pyramid that adults have been doing for the past couple of years?

How could you have *missed* it? It's supposed to be the new way we can figure out what we're supposed to eat. We're supposed to look at the pyramid and see that the pointy part on top has Fats in it. Then we're supposed to say to ourselves, "Oh. Fats only make up the little pointy part of the pyramid, so we're not supposed to eat very many fats."

Meanwhile, down at the big, thick bottom of the pyramid, there are lots of Grains and Cereals. So we're supposed to think, "Ah. We should eat big amounts of grains and cereals." Totally ignoring the fact that we are humans, not fodder-eating work animals.

Anyway, junior high school students—who do not go for big amounts of grain—have a food pyramid of their own. It looks like this:

111

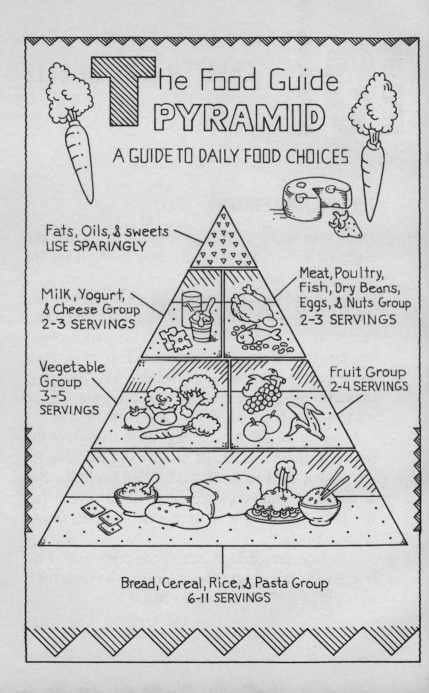

The Food Guide
PYRAMID
A GUIDE TO DAILY FOOD CHOICES

Fats, Oils, & sweets
USE SPARINGLY

Milk, Yogurt,
& Cheese Group
2-3 SERVINGS

Meat, Poultry,
Fish, Dry Beans,
Eggs, & Nuts Group
2-3 SERVINGS

Vegetable
Group
3-5
SERVINGS

Fruit Group
2-4 SERVINGS

Bread, Cereal, Rice, & Pasta Group
6-11 SERVINGS

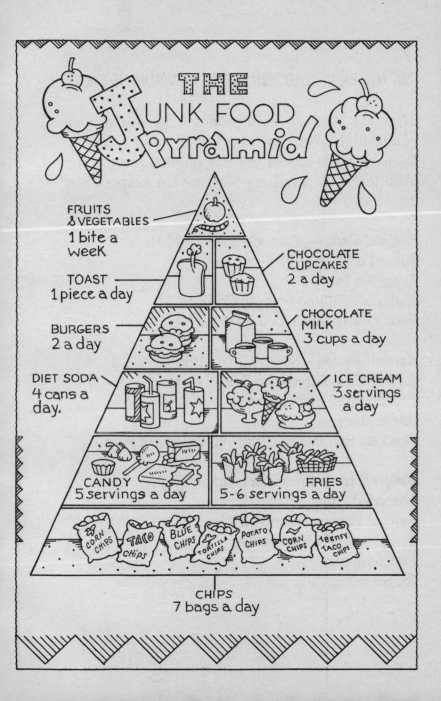

THE FIVE WORST CAFETERIA MENUS IN THE UNITED STATES

How can reading these menus help you survive junior high? Well, at least they'll keep you from transferring to any of the schools that serve them. And that will go a long way toward keeping you healthy.

Oriental Medley—East-West Junior High
Liver Lo Mein
Won Ton Paste
Coleslaw-Stuffed Fortune Cookies
Fruit Gelatin Sprinkled w/ Fried Noodles

Catch o' the Sea—Sandy Cove Middle School
Baked Things-from-the-Sea-Bottom
French Fried Fish Scales
Algae Bites
Octopus Eye Pudding with Whipped Topping

Budget D-Lite—Cheapskate Junior High
Shredded Paper Salad
Salt 'n' Pepper Toast with Water Sauce
The Emperor's New Roast
Pan Scrapings
Ice Sorbet

Fiesta Olé!—San Jose Junior High
Rain-from-Spain Soup
Donkey Tacos w/ Pineapple Salsa
Burrito-like Food
Food-like Burritos
Phlegm Flan

Dairy Treet—Elsie Country Day School
*Mmmmmmm*Milkburgers
Curdled Egg Soup
Buttered Margarine Sticks
Cheese Fries

OTHER USES FOR LUNCHROOM FOOD

Now, we're not going to make any bad-cafeteria-food jokes here. We swear we're not. It's been done to death—by us, among other people.

We'd just like to point out that some of the food they serve in your lunchroom can be used for a lot more (or less) than food. Contrary to what the lunch ladies may say, this isn't playing with your food. Finding new ways to use food helps avoid waste. It also keeps you busy, which improves your brainpower. So roll up your sleeves and dig in!

Lunchroom Food	New Use
Mashed Potatoes	Paste cracks in cafeteria ceiling
Carrot Sticks	Build ladder to help you reach ceiling
Fruit Gelatin	Cut into extra-thin slivers and sell as contact lenses
Canned Corn	Glue on pierced-earring backs and make attractive earrings for holiday gifts
Chocolate Pudding	Plant moss on top and put into terrarium
Ham Slice	Toss around as a Frisbee
Cream of Tomato Soup	Fake blood for Halloween costume
Cream of Mushroom Soup	Fake barf for April Fool's Day
Tuna Melt	Replace roofing tiles
Chicken Nuggets	Golf balls for idiots
Oven-Fried Goat	Fill empty trash barrels and toss out

THE DON'TS OF YOUR CAFETERIA

Manners are important everywhere you go, except in your school cafeteria. No, just kidding. They're important there, too. In fact, they're more important there than anywhere else. Except for Andrew Jackson, our nation's presidents all had excellent cafeteria manners. (In fact, George Washington was called "First in the hearts of his countrymen" because he always let his countrymen go ahead of him in the lunch line.)

So memorize these simple rules—and start packing for Washington.

1. Do not use your lunch tray as a Frisbee when there is food on it.

2. Do not blow bubbles with your straw unless you are scuba-diving in your milk.

3. Do not throw any food that has sauce on it, as this might stain the clothes of an innocent passerby.

4. Do not shoot chocolate pudding up to the cafeteria ceiling. It will pick up ceiling dust and not taste as good when it falls.

5. Do not use a fish stick as a bookmark.

6. Do not eat off anyone else's tray unless they are

not looking.

7. Do not put mustard and ketchup on your ice cream sandwich. Use one or the other.

8. Do not say "You gotta be kidding!" when the lady dishing out the cafeteria food tells you it is lasagna.

9. Do not use your sleeve to wipe your mouth. What do you think your neighbor's sleeve is for?

10. Do not put your gum on your tray while you eat lunch. Put your gum on your tray *before* you eat lunch.

11

THE DIRTY TRUTH ABOUT AFTER-SCHOOL ACTIVITIES

THE BASICS

For some kids, after-school activities are the reason you suffer through school in the first place. For others, the only worthwhile after-school activity is watching reruns of *Flipper* on TV.

Unfortunately, few schools have Watching Reruns of *Flipper* Clubs. Would you settle for the Ham Radio Club? No? Then get out of our faces until you find some school spirit.

A good junior high has an after-school activity for every student. Here are a few basics all junior high schools should offer:

Every major intramural sport, including Fencing,
   Table Tennis, and Luge
Drama Club
Cheerleading
Student Newspaper
Mixed Chorus

French Club
Spanish Club
Finnish Club
Future Doctors of America
Future Lawyers of America
Future Mall Rats of America
Time Travelers
Junior Varsity Goldfish Fanciers
I Hate Mustard Club
Debating Without Getting the Giggles Club
Girls Who Still Love Horses Society
Kids Whose Parents Sometimes Swear
Celtic Folk Dancing
Accordion-Lovers' Club
Hall Hikers
Cast-Signers' Club
Pig Latin Club
Pig Sanskrit Club
We're Just Hanging Around in the Media Center
   Waiting for the Late Bus Club
Young Raisin Growers of America
The Chocolate Eaters' Society
Proud of My C– Minus Club
Shoe-Tying Around the World
Any Excuse for a Bake Sale Guild
Junior Varsity Jesters
The Ye-Olders of Yore

Ham Radio Club
Bacon TV Club
Coin Collecting Club
Coin Spending Club

We sincerely hope your school offers all of these and more. If it doesn't, you're being cheated. Complain to the school board.

SO YOU WANT TO BE A CHEERLEADER? THEN DON'T USE THESE CHEERS!

Two bits! Four bits! Six bits! A dollar!
My little puppy has a bright red collar!
He's always scratching 'round for fleas,
And when I take him out he —
Who do we want? HO-Bart!
Who do we want? HO-Bart!
> —The Hobartettes of Middle Creek Junior High got in a lot of trouble for this one, even though they claimed they hadn't meant anything by it.

What do we want? HALFTIME!
When do we want it? NOW!
> —This was penned by the North Woods Junior High School Pep Team, who lost their pep when it started to rain.

Colgate, Aqua-Fresh, and Crest,
The Dedham Dentists are the best!
We drill, we scrape, we go for pain.
Guess what? We don't use Novocain!
GOOOOOO, DENTISTS!

>—The Dedham Junior High Cheering Squad wrote this ingenious number. Unfortunately, they got the name of their team wrong. It is the Dedham *Diggsters,* not Dentists.

We know your moms are watching,
This means a lot to you.
And though we'd really love to win,
We know you'd love to, too.
So here's a little tip for you,
Don't tell our team we told:
Kick it up the middle,
'Cause the halfback has a cold.

>—The Red Raiders' cheerleading team was notorious for always feeling sorry for the other team. After this cheer lost the game for the Raiders, cheerleading was banned at the school for two years.

Thunder! Thunderation!
We're the Chess Team generation!
When we yell with determination!
We're kicked out of the tourna-mation!

—Cheering at the Chester Junior High Chess Team tournaments turned out not to be such a good idea after all.

We're mighty tense 'round here,
But there's one thing we know:
Chester Gunlock can really bat,
So therefore we have nothing to worry about!
HEY!

—The Lafayette Pep Squad *meant* well. It wasn't their fault that they were totally rhyme-deaf.

SCHOOL PICTURES: TORTURE OR INHUMANE CRUELTY?

Whatever club, sport, or activity you do after school, the dreaded day always comes when you have to have your picture taken for the yearbook. That means the photographer will spend about thirty hours arranging you all by height, and for the first time the whole group will notice how much shorter you are than everyone else. And when the photographer finally takes your picture, you will all blink.

To save your time and everyone else's, we've compiled a few simple instructions for what you should be doing when your picture is taken. And take off that stupid baseball cap!

Football Team: Squint into the sun. Look angry. Hold your helmets facing front so that they look like skulls. Show one shot of someone from another team getting stepped on by someone on your team.

Basketball Team: Have one shot of just a lot of hands clutching at the ball; have another shot of the audience gasping as an incredible basket is made. For the group shot, everyone should be kneeling on their right knee except for Luke Santorelli, who always makes such a big thing about having a bad knee.

Soccer Team: Whatever else you do, make sure one picture shows a lot of people wallowing around in the mud.

Glee Club: Show as many people as possible with their mouths wide open. This will make their necks look thick and bullish.

French Club: The club must be posed in front of a picture of the Eiffel Tower, and everyone must be wearing a beret. *There are no exceptions.*

Drama Society: Don't smile for the group shot. This will show that you are all serious actors. Always include a picture from one musical—

preferably with someone singing while spit sprays out of her mouth—and one picture from an "important" play—preferably showing the audience in the background looking really bored.

School Newspaper: The group shot has to be comical. For instance, one staff member should be typing with her feet, while another pretends to snooze with a newspaper over his head and a third tries to sharpen a quill pen. To balance this picture, there should be a shot of the whole staff having a big argument with the faculty adviser about whether to run that article criticizing the eighth-grade dance.

12

WHAT TO DO AFTER THE BUDGET CUTS

AFTER-SCHOOL ACTIVITIES YOU CAN DO ON YOUR OWN

Now that you've discovered what fun after-school activities can be, guess what? They've all been canceled!

That's right. The money is running out for your junior high school. Every year, the adults in your community get to vote on how much money to spend in taxes on public education. And every year, they vote to spend a little less than the year before.

"Who cares about kids?" aging adults all over the country are starting to ask. "Ours are grown up. Why shouldn't we spend money on a new golf cart instead of schools?"

"Hey, good point!" students all over the country are *not* replying.

When after-school budgets are cut, after-school activities are usually the first to go. But that's not necessarily bad news. There are literally tons of ways you can spend your spare time . . . *and* have fun that almost seems real.

When field hockey is cut, how about replacing it with hopscotch? You'll save even more money if you scrape your grid on the pavement with a pebble instead of wasting valuable chalk!

Do you miss the keen competition of the debating team? Well, replace it with a Count-the-Coat-Hanger contest in the Teachers' Lounge. Your competitive spirit will be fanned into flame!

Another great (and cheap!) competition: Count Your Sneezes. This one is done on the honor system, making it even more suspenseful.

Varsity Stair-Climbing costs a lot less than Cross-Country, and it's better for your heart.

Yes, it was fun being in all those Glee Club concerts at other schools. But now that Glee Club has been cut, you finally have the time to sing "A Billion Bottles of Beer on the Wall" from start to finish!

Have a school-wide scavenger hunt! Can you find: a chipped floor tile, a broken locker door, a desk with no leg? There are lots of signs that your school is falling apart.

Chemistry Club is gone, but you and your friends won't miss it when you form an Identify-

That-Smell Club in your cafeteria.

You won't miss Art Club, either. Watching paint peel off the school walls combines the fun of art *and* TV.

No more Ski Club? Great! Now you're free to ski down the stairs with lunch trays taped to your feet.

And Wastebasket Basketball is even more exciting than the real kind, because you get to make the ball yourself, out of crumpled-up paper!

AFTER THE BUDGET CUTS, PART 2: NEW NAMES FOR OLD ROOMS

"It was too depressing calling places by their old names once they'd been cut from the budget and we couldn't use them anymore," recalls Vice-Principal Rodney Thwipperson of Needalot Junior High. "So we had a brainstorming session to change the names. Now we're all feeling more positive because we feel more negative."

It might work for your school, too. Take a look:

Old Name	New Name
Music Room	Music Museum
Swimming Pool	The Big Empty
Chemistry Lab	Frankenstein's Lair

Biology Lab	Formaldehyde Stinker
Language Lab	Tower of Babble
Home Ec Kitchen	Lunchroom II
Art Center	Mess Hall
Media Center	Place of Dead Authors

THE WONDERFUL WORLD OF MAKING DO

Sometimes a school has to do more to save money than just rename a few media enters. Sometimes money must be saved by—uh—*saving money*. As their budgets get "slasheder and slasheder," junior high schools everywhere are learning to make do.

If you really care about your school (no wisecracks here, please), then you will be interested in helping your school save money so that it can survive the budget cuts and still offer you a top education (no wisecracks here, either).

Here are some cost-saving ideas you might want to suggest to your principal, if he or she hasn't been cut from the budget:

1. Buy the economy size. Two small bottles of dishwashing detergent are more expensive than one large-sized, right? So, you can save money by buying one giant blackboard and then cutting it up into little blackboards. You might want to try this with one giant teacher, too.

2. Always ask yourself: "Do we really need this?" Do you really need to use *all* the numbers? Wouldn't 1 through 5 do? Think of all the money you could save by eliminating 6 through 10. Your school might want to cut back on vowels. Or eliminate ink altogether—instead of writing memos and reports, just imagine them!

3. Generic teachers can teach just about anything—from Math to Choir to Home Ec to the alphabet. Many cost only pennies per class.

4. "Field Trips OUT. Fantasy IN!" should be your new motto. Imaginary field trips can be even more boring than real ones! Just close your eyes and *think* about your class slowly filing through the Post Office or the local printing shop. Isn't that even better than being there?

5. Make use of nature. Students at Schagticoke Junior High wowed their friends by learning to get along without paper after taxpayers cut the annual Schagticoke budget to fifty cents. "We make paper out of birch bark now," explained Clayton Parks, a Schagticoke eighth grader. "Everyone gets one piece a year. We have to use it for tissues, too—so it really cuts down on colds."

6. Fifty kids per class? Hey, it's one big party! You can sit on each others' laps!

7. Teacher layoffs are a great way to catch up on your sleep. One school in Irondequoit, New York, replaced Algebra with Study Hall, Geometry with Rest Time, American History with Silent Thought, and Biology with Thinking Hard. The school is much more peaceful now.

8. Everything must go! Have a schoolwide garage sale. Sell all those things that no one uses anyway, like textbooks and the gym floor and those big pans in the cafeteria. Or try selling the teachers' cars while the teachers are having a faculty meeting. Try selling your teachers, too.

9. There was going to be a number 9, but it was cut from the budget.

10. Save wear and tear on your desk. Stay home.

13

AND FURTHERMORE . . . IMPORTANT THINGS TO REMEMBER

YOUR JUNIOR HIGH GLOSSARY

Angles—Cornery things that must be measured, for some reason. Acute angles are adorable. Obtuse angles are so stupid that sometimes they don't even know they're angles. They think they're planes. Right angles are never wrong and brag all the time.

Assembly—Spitball practice time. Highest points awarded to a spitter who hits the speaker.

Atom—Don't worry about atoms. You can never see one no matter how hard you look.

Calisthenics—What gym teachers call aerobics, plus jumping jacks.

Cheerleaders—People who have to practice jumping and yelling—activities that come naturally to everybody else.

Cleats—A very, very ugly kind of shoe with thumbtacks that are supposed to keep you from falling in the mud.

ASSEMBLY

Compass—A sharp weapon that they give you in math class to try to draw circles with, only the pencil always bounces.

Congruent—Fancy word for "equal," used to show off.

Cosine—Almost like a sine, but a little more "co."

Cumulus—The clouds you used to draw when you were in elementary school.

Demerits—Dese liddle tiny t'ings dat youse gets when youse is a liddle bit bad.

Detention—Da big punishment dat youse gets when youse gets too many demerits.

Digestive system—Gross! We don't even want to *think* about it!

Fire drill—An excuse to mill around in the front yard of the school; also an excuse for teachers to say, "Single file, no talking!"

Gravity—A law of nature, even if the police don't care if you break it.

Hamburger—What the cafeteria ladies call those elephant scabs they serve "on a bun."

Health class—The code words for learning stuff you don't want to talk to your parents about.

Home ec—A class where you learn to make a blouse that looks like a pillowcase.

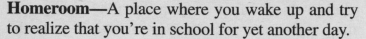

Homeroom—A place where you wake up and try to realize that you're in school for yet another day.

Horse—A much too tall, stupid object that they make you try to jump over so you will be humiliated when you fall. Note: Do not feed oats to this so-called "horse."

Lever—A way to lift heavy things when you're too weak to pick them up.

Magna Charta—Something that was signed in England a long time ago and took away some of the king's power, or something. Nowadays they do not make magna chartas that you can use against teachers.

Molecule—Something little, but not as little as the atom!

Passes—Pieces of paper you try to get that let you do anything.

Plane—A big flat thing that you have to know about even though it's imaginary.

Ponce de León—Wasn't he the one who was looking for the fountain of youth? Or was that just an excuse to go to Florida?

Protractor—From the Latin, "for the tractor." It measures angles (see *Angles*)—like you really need to know that in real life!

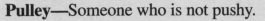

Pulley—Someone who is not pushy.

Relief map—A map you make with bumps. We never got any relief from it, though.

Semicolon—What you use when you're too cheap to use a whole colon.

Shop—They call it a shop, but it's really the opposite. In a real shop, you get to buy stuff for money. In shop, you have to make stuff to give away for free.

Social Studies—Nothing to do with your social life, unfortunately.

Stamp Act—One of the seven things you always put down when they ask for the causes of the Revolutionary War. Today, it would be known as the FedEx Act.

Street clothes—What gym teachers call regular clothes. Maybe gym teachers think you spend the rest of your school day on the street. Are there road clothes?

Study hall—From the Latin "Studius hallius," meaning "a place for merriment, note-passing, and eating food that you keep hidden under your desk."

Theme—Themes are hard to explain, so we're going to show you with an example. If you write the sentence, "Johnny Tremain burned his hand," the *theme* of the sentence is "A Young Boy Grows into Manhood During the Revolutionary War."

Topic sentence—Well, it has to have a topic and be a sentence. And you have to find it somewhere in the paragraph or you will get a lower grade.

Vector—Hey, don't ask us!

Verb—They call it the action word, but *we* never saw it go anywhere.

ALL THE THINGS YOU'LL NEVER MAKE YOUR KIDS DO WHEN THEY'RE IN JUNIOR HIGH

Okay. You're surviving junior high school.

Someday you'll survive high school, and someday you'll have your own children. And *they* will go to junior high.

Will your kids have the rough time that you had? Will they have to wear gym suits that scrape the ground and listen to Miss Pennypacker's rings clank against the blackboard and die of embarrassment every time their parents come into the room? It's up to you.

If you really care about your kids, you'll memorize this handy list. It will help you become an understanding parent—the kind of parent who gives their kids so many survival skills that the kids will never need to read a book like this.

I promise to write my kids notes excusing them from their homework.

I promise to say my kids are not home when people they don't like call and ask them over.

I promise never to open my mouth at a PTA meeting.

I promise to agree when my kids make fun of their teacher.

I promise never to tell cute stories about the time my kids took off their clothes in the grocery store.

I promise to pretend I am not related to my kids whenever we are out in public.

I promise to let my kids go to movies on important holidays, even Christmas Eve.

I promise never to say, "You know, I was your age once."

I promise never to ask my kids who they danced with when they go to a school dance.

I promise to let them have whatever kind of hair/earrings/pierced nose/tattoos/clothes/plastic surgery they want, whenever they want it.

I promise to take care of all the pets my children said they would be responsible for, and never say "I told you so."

I promise never to make my kids try to understand

why obnoxious kids act obnoxious, and just let them hate these kids if they want to.

I promise never to ask, "Isn't this a school night?"

I promise that if I am the driver in a carpool, I will sit in utter silence as I drive.

I promise never to appear in a bathrobe in front of my kids' friends.

I promise never to be as gross and old-looking as my parents.

I promise never to make my kids go to junior high.

P.S. ON THE OTHER HAND . . .
DO YOU REALLY NEED JUNIOR HIGH?
THESE FAMOUS PEOPLE MANAGED JUST FINE WITHOUT IT!

Benjamin Franklin was so busy being a printer's apprentice that he never had time to enroll at the local junior high (which, coincidentally, was called Benjamin Franklin Junior High). As a result, he never learned to come in out of the rain. This led to his discovery of electricity. Just think, if Franklin *had* gone to junior high, we'd probably still be using battery-powered TVs.

Zeus, the leader of the Greek gods, never had the time to go to junior high either. "Who cares?" he once said when his wife, Hera, was teasing him

about it. "I can throw thunderbolts a million times better than those ninth-grade geeks." To which Hera answered, "Sticks and thunderbolts may break my bones, but words can never hurt me."

Young *Abraham Lincoln* was too tall to get inside his one-room junior high school. He stayed at home and studied in his one-room cabin instead, resting his head against the rafters. "I never learned any football cheers," Lincoln admitted later with his characteristic dry wit. "On the other hand, I never had my lunch money stolen by eighth graders either." Later, Lincoln was able to use the lunch money he'd saved to buy votes for his first senatorial campaign.

Some wicked animals persuaded *Pinocchio* to quit junior high and become an actor instead—a fate kids of today can really identify with. Now, it's true that Pinocchio did grow donkey ears and get swallowed by a fish after that, which maybe wasn't the greatest luck. But if you saw the movie, you'll remember that he still turned into a boy at the end anyway. So obviously school had nothing to do with it.

When *Florence Nightingale* was young, girls of her social class did not attend junior high schools, but were tutored at home by governesses instead. Nightingale never let this get in the way of her ambitions. She became a nurse in the Crimean War. On the battlefields she changed the face of nursing and learned from the soldiers all the swear words she would have learned from ninth graders if she'd had the chance to go to junior high.

Sleeping Beauty slept through all four years of junior high. It didn't matter, though, because she was just a character in a fairy tale.

Unfortunately, you are not.